READING ABOUT

Tornadoes

Anna Claybourne

Aladdin/Watts
London • Sydney

Contents

1 What Is a Tornado?   **page 3**
How Big Are They? • What Tornadoes Look Like

2 How Tornadoes Begin   **page 8**
Thunderstorms • Spinning Air • How Fast Are They?

3 What Tornadoes Do   **page 13**
Danger • Damage • Strange Colours • Sounds

4 Tornado Alley   **page 17**
Where Tornadoes Happen • Disasters

5 Keeping Safe   **page 21**
Get Underground • Cars Aren't Safe

6 Tornado Tales   **page 24**
Waterspouts • Dust Devils • Skyfalls

7 Storm-Chasers   **page 27**
Tornado Science • Measuring Speed

Find Out More   **page 30**

Index and Picture Answers   **page 32**

© Aladdin Books Ltd 2000

Designed and produced by
Aladdin Books Ltd
28 Percy Street
London W1P 0LD

First published in
Great Britain in 2000 by
Franklin Watts
96 Leonard Street
London EC2A 4XD

ISBN 0 7496 3437 5
A catalogue record for this
book is available from the
British Library.

Printed in Belgium
All rights reserved

Editor
Jim Pipe

Scientific Consultant
Prof. Derek M. Elsom, Tornado and
Storm Research Organisation (TORRO)

Series Literacy Consultant
Wendy Cobb

Design
Flick Killerby Book Design and Graphics

Picture Research
Brooks Krikler Research

What Is a Tornado?

How Big Are They? • What Tornadoes Look Like

A tornado is a type of wind storm. In fact, it's the windiest sort of wind storm there is. The winds of a tornado can smash windows and lift people and cars into the air.

Tornadoes are very scary. The dark, spinning clouds appear suddenly and with a big roar like a jet plane. The only safe place to hide is underground, in a cellar or a shelter.

The film *Twister* showed how scary tornadoes are.

Tornadoes aren't very big next to other storms. A thunderstorm can be several kilometres wide. Very big storms, called hurricanes, are often 500 km from one side to the other.

The largest tornadoes are only about 2 km wide. Most are even smaller. They don't travel very fast and many appear for only a short time.

Hurricanes are so big they can be seen from space.

So why are tornadoes so scary? How do they cause so much damage?

Instead of moving across the land in a straight line, the wind in a tornado twists round and round. So all the winds in a tornado happen in one small area. This makes them very powerful.

A tornado is like the shape that you see when water goes down a plughole. But it's much bigger, and made out of air instead of water.

You can tell what tornadoes are like by the names people call them. They are known as "twisters", "cyclones" and "whirlwinds".

This tornado looks like a giant elephant's trunk.

A tornado is made of winds twisting round and round in a long, tall tower. As a tornado gets narrower, it spins faster and faster.

The top of a tornado sucks dark storm clouds down from the sky. They swirl around in the tornado and make it look dark at the top.

The bottom of the tornado moves along the ground. If the tornado is strong, it smashes everything it touches. It picks up dust and rubbish and carries them along. This makes a tornado look dark at the bottom.

One storm can make lots of tornadoes. You can never tell where the next tornado is going to happen.

How Tornadoes Begin

Thunderstorms • Spinning Air • How Fast Are They?

Tornadoes don't happen by themselves. First, there has to be a thunderstorm. Even the word "tornado" comes from "tronada", the Spanish word for thunderstorm.

But not all thunderstorms turn into tornadoes. Everything has to be just right for a tornado to start.

There is always a thunderstorm before a tornado.

A tornado begins when warm air meets cold air inside a thunderstorm. The cold air sinks down and the warm air zooms up.

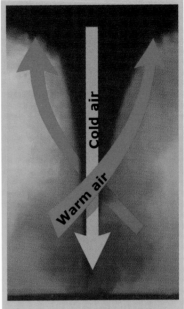

Cold air

Warm air

In a tornado, cold air sinks down. The warm air spins up.

This happens because cold air is heavier than warm air. The warm, light air bounces to the top, like air bubbles in a bath.

As the warm air moves upwards it starts to twist around in a spiral. Scientists think this happens because of the way the Earth spins.

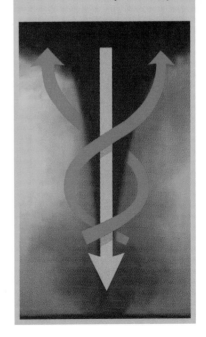

Now the tornado starts to grow.

Air gets sucked into the tornado. The tornado gets longer and longer until it reaches the ground.

As the warm air spins upwards it sucks more and more air in with it. As the cold air pushes downwards, the tornado stretches out towards the ground. It makes a long funnel shape.

When a wide tornado gets narrower, it twists around faster. The same thing happens with ice skaters.

You see skaters spinning round on the ice with both arms sticking out. Then they bring their arms in and suddenly spin much faster.

Once the tornado has reached the ground, it doesn't stay still. It moves along the ground. But it is still joined to the clouds above it.

A tornado usually travels at about 55 km/h. That's not very fast. You can drive much faster in a car. But the winds spinning around inside the tornado are very fast — up to 500 km/h.

Some tornadoes travel only a few metres. Others go on for hundreds of kilometres.

When a strong tornado comes your way, incredibly fast winds whizz past for a few minutes. That's long enough for a tornado to destroy everything in its path.

Eventually, the tornado dies away as the air inside gets cooler and stops rising upwards. Most tornadoes only last for a few minutes. The longest last for about an hour.

Some people try to drive away from tornadoes. This is very dangerous.

What Tornadoes Do

Danger • Damage • Strange Colours • Sounds

The effects of a tornado can be amazing! Some tornadoes are so strong and powerful they can lift things right up into the air, carry them a long way, then drop them down somewhere else.

All the things being carried by a tornado spin round very fast too. So if you're caught in a tornado, you get blasted by the winds — and hit by flying objects as well.

What made this fork stick into the tree? The answer is on page 32.

Tornadoes throw objects with great force and make it very dangerous to go outside. One tornado buried a spade 15 cm deep in a tree trunk.

Cars roll over and over in the strong winds. Powerful tornadoes can blow the roof off a house and break the windows in your home.

Tornadoes can lift up all kinds of things — not just people, but boats, cows and even trains, as well as lots of smaller things.

This car rolled over in a tornado.

Here are some amazing things that tornadoes have moved:

In 1954, in Wisconsin, United States, a tornado lifted up a dog and carried it away. Four hours later, the dog came walking home.

In 1992, in Peking, China, a tornado carried a nine-year-old girl 3 km, but she wasn't hurt by the ride!

In 1895, in Iowa, United States, two horses were lifted up to a height of 300 m. They looked like specks in the sky. Then the tornado dropped them and they fell to the ground.

A tornado in England in 1950 left a flock of chickens without their feathers! The wind had plucked them all out.

Tornadoes don't just do terrible things. They look and sound scary too. First, the sky turns a very dark green. As it grows, the tornado makes a rushing, hissing sound. Then it roars loudly as it whizzes across the land.

The sky often turns a strange colour during a tornado.

Tornado Alley

Many of the tornadoes shown in this book happened in North America.

Tornadoes can happen almost anywhere. But the big, dangerous ones are usually in the middle of the United States.

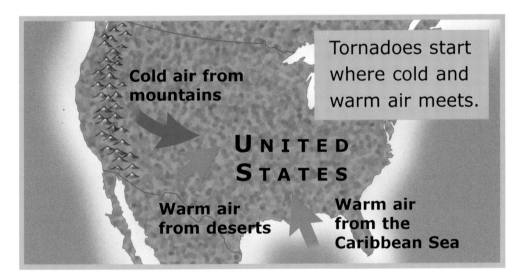

Cold air from mountains

Tornadoes start where cold and warm air meets.

UNITED STATES

Warm air from deserts

Warm air from the Caribbean Sea

In this area, warm air blowing from the deserts and the Caribbean Sea meets cold air blowing from the mountains. This helps to cause tornadoes, because they start when warm and cold air are mixed together.

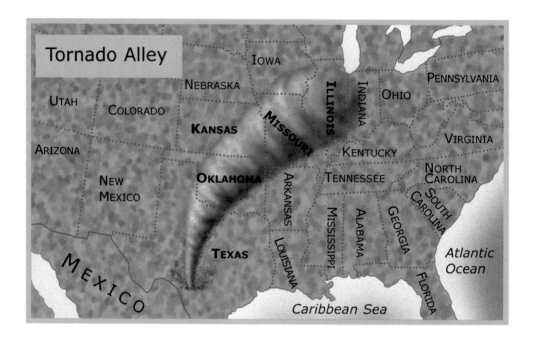

The worst area for tornadoes is called "Tornado Alley". It stretches across the states of Texas, Oklahoma, Missouri, Kansas and Illinois.

The tornadoes here are worst in spring, and every year they kill over 50 people.

The biggest tornado disaster ever was on March 18, 1925. Nearly 700 people died and over 2,000 were injured when a very big tornado roared from Missouri to Illinois.

This tornado moved at 100 km/h and ripped apart the town of Gorham. In Murphysboro, three schools fell down, and many people were hit by the falling walls.

Tornadoes happen in other places too. A strong one hit the city of Perth, in Australia, in July 1996.

There are about 35 tornadoes each year in Great Britain. But most are very weak.

A tornado destroyed this family's home.

Not all tornadoes are strong. But it is dangerous to stand near even weak ones.

Keeping Safe

The biggest danger in a tornado is getting hit by flying objects. So if a tornado strikes, the most important things to do are: GET INSIDE and GET UNDERGROUND!

Not all houses are safe. A tornado has ripped the roof off this home.

If you can, hide in a cellar and wait for the tornado to go past. If you don't have a cellar:

- Get under the stairs or go to an inside room on the lowest floor of your house.
- Hide under a heavy table or mattress.
- Try to protect your head.

Cars aren't safe. Half the people killed in recent tornadoes were hiding in cars or mobile homes.

However, scientists say that many people still do the wrong things in a tornado. Here are some of the things you should never do:

 Never try to drive away from the tornado to escape. Cars can go faster than most tornadoes. But a tornado might "hop" and land right on top of you!

 Don't open any windows! Open windows just let in more flying objects that could hit someone.

Never hide under a bridge. Wind goes even faster as it zooms through spaces like the gap under a bridge.

Some people believe they are safe because tornadoes never hit city centres or towns between two rivers! They're wrong. The truth is, tornadoes can strike anywhere.

Tornadoes can happen in cities too!

Tornado Tales

Waterspouts • Dust Devils • Skyfalls

There are some very strange stories and odd beliefs about tornadoes.

Sometimes tornadoes form over the sea. Instead of sucking up dust and dirt, they suck up water in a long tube called a waterspout.

Long ago, sailors used to be afraid of waterspouts. But most of them are not dangerous.

In the past, people thought waterspouts were sea monsters.

Spinning winds in the desert are called "dust devils". They suck up sand in a tower 1,000 m high, and whizz across the land.

Desert peoples called dust devils "genies". They thought they were magic spirits.

Tornadoes also appear in stories. In *The Wizard of Oz*, a tornado lifts up Dorothy's house and carries it to the land of Oz. A few tornadoes really are strong enough to lift up a house. That's why the cellar is the best place to hide.

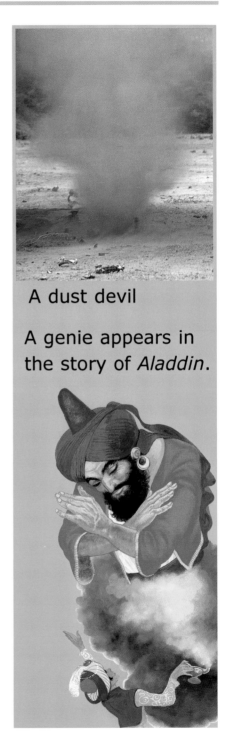

A dust devil

A genie appears in the story of *Aladdin*.

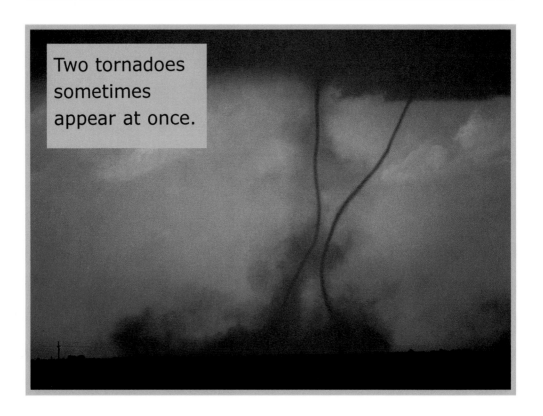

Two tornadoes sometimes appear at once.

One of the most amazing things that can happen after a tornado is a skyfall. In a skyfall, it rains frogs, fish, or sometimes even bigger animals like sheep.

People used to think skyfalls were magical. But the animals probably got sucked up and then carried by a strong tornado.

Storm-Chasers

Scientists still don't really know exactly how tornadoes work. It's hard to work out why some storms create a tornado and others don't.

One reason for this is that it's not very easy to follow tornadoes. Even though it's very dangerous, some scientists do follow tornadoes in cars. This is called storm-chasing.

Cameras in space follow the storms that make tornadoes.

Storm-chasers take photos of tornadoes and watch how they start and move.

Some scientists used to measure tornadoes by leaving a machine called TOTO in their path. This was named after Dorothy's dog from the story, *The Wizard of Oz*.

Other scientists collected the junk left by a tornado. Then they tried to work out how far it had been carried. This helped them tell how fast and strong a tornado was.

Scientists today use a machine called Doppler Radar to measure the speed of a tornado.

One radar measured a tornado with winds moving at over 510 km/h.

If you are worried, remember that this book talks about the strongest tornadoes. Most of them are very weak. You'd be very unlucky to get hit.

Find Out More

PICTURE QUIZ

Can you think of six things that can happen in a tornado? Look at the pictures below for some clues. They can all be found in this book. The answers are on page 32.

UNUSUAL WORDS

Here we explain some words you may have read in this book.

Cyclone Another name for a tornado.

Debris Junk, dust and broken objects. Tornadoes pick up lots of debris and blow it around.

Dust devil A tornado in the desert which picks up sand in its funnel.

Funnel The long, narrow V-shape made by a twisting tornado.

Gale A very strong wind.

Hurricane A very big windstorm.

Radar A machine that uses radio waves to track objects in the sky.

A skyfall of frogs

Skyfall A shower of animals instead of rain. The animals are picked up by a tornado.

Storm-chasing Chasing after a tornado in a car or truck.

Storm shelter A special room dug in the ground, for hiding in during a tornado.

Tronada This Spanish word for thunderstorm gave us the English word "tornado".

Twister Another name for a tornado, especially a very strong one.

Waterspout A tornado over the sea that sucks up water into its funnel.

Whirlwind Another name for a tornado.

Worst Tornado Attacks

In 1989, a tornado in Bangladesh in southern Asia left about 1,300 people dead and at least 30,000 homeless. In 1974, 148 tornadoes hit towns from Alabama to Michigan over a few hours.

STRANGE TORNADOES
Waterspouts

Waterspouts can happen over lakes or seas. Some of them cause strong winds and can damage ships. But many are harmless. Usually they are about 450 m high, but some are 900 m tall.

Dust Devils

Dust devils look like tornadoes but they are not caused by storm clouds. They happen when hot air rising from the desert is spun around by winds higher up.

Sisters

When tornadoes appear in pairs they are called "sisters". When many tornadoes appear at about the same time, they are called a "swarm".

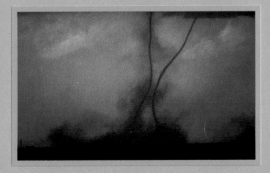

Index

Air currents 9, 10, 17
Alabama 31
Australia 19

Bangladesh 31
Britain 25

Caribbean Sea 17
China 15
Clouds 3, 6, 11, 31
Colours 16
Cyclones 5, 30

Damage 13, 14, 18, 19, 21, 22, 31
Debris 30
Desert 17, 25, 30, 31
Dust devils 25, 30, 31

Films
  The Wizard of Oz 25, 28
  Twister 3

Funnel 10, 30

Genies 25
Gorham 19

Hurricanes 4, 30

Illinois 18

Kansas 18

Michigan 31
Missouri 18
Murphysboro 19

Oklahoma 18

Perth 19

Radar 29, 30

Safety 21, 22
Skyfalls 26, 30

Sounds 3, 12, 16
Storm-chasing 27, 28, 30
Storms 3, 4, 27, 31
Storm shelter 21, 22, 23

Texas 18
Thunderstorms 4, 8, 9, 30
Tornado Alley 17, 18
TOTO 28
Tronada 8, 30
Twisters 5, 30

United States 15, 17

Waterspouts 24, 30, 31
Whirlwinds 5, 30
Winds 3, 5, 6, 11, 12, 13, 14, 23, 25, 29, 30, 31

ANSWERS TO PICTURE QUESTIONS

Page 12 It is *not* a good idea to escape a tornado by driving away. A car will not protect you if a tornado catches up with it.
Page 13 Tornado winds have flung the fork so hard that it has stuck into a tree trunk.

Page 30 Six things that happen in a tornado are: **1** The sky changes colour. **2** Cars are blown over. **3** Objects are flung about by the winds. **4** Roofs are blown off houses. **5** Winds pick up people and animals. **6** A roaring sound.

Illustrators: Pete Roberts – Allied Artists; Stephen Sweet – SGA; Francis Phillips.
Photocredits: *Abbreviations: t-top, m-middle, b-bottom, r-right, l-left, c-centre.* Pages 4, 6, 7, 11, 13, 25, 26, 27, 30cl, 31m & b – Oxford Scientific Films; 1, 3, 10b, 12, 16, 19, 21, 23, 24, 28-29, 30l & r & 31t – Rex Features; 2t, 8, 10t, 14, 20, 22 & 30cr – Frank Spooner Pictures.